Beyond Profit

Evelyn Wright

Legal and legal data
Copyright holder: © Sebastian MG
Author: © Evelyn Wright
Year: 2024

Index

Evelyn Wright

The New Paradigm of Success

In the history of business, success has traditionally been measured by a single factor: profits. This simplified and often short-sighted approach has dominated the minds of entrepreneurs, managers and investors for generations. In economics books, in business classrooms, and in everyday conversations about business, the concept of success has been reduced to a simple mathematical equation: maximize profits at all costs. But, in these times, this paradigm is being questioned like never before.

Today, more people are realizing that defining success solely by the numbers on the bottom line is a limited and, in many cases, destructive view. It's not that profits don't matter; of course. Companies must be profitable to survive and grow. But when profit becomes the only objective, other crucial factors become forgotten. What about the environmental impact of a company's operations? What about the way you treat your employees, your suppliers, or even the communities in which you operate? These aspects, as vital as profits, have been ignored for too long.

The new paradigm of business success proposes a radical change in how we define what it means to be successful. It's no longer just about making money; it's about doing it in a way that also benefits society and the planet. This new approach recognizes that companies are part of a broader ecosystem and that their actions have repercussions that go beyond their office doors. Thus, success is not only measured in dollars or euros, but also in terms of social and environmental impact.

Let's consider for a moment a company that has decided to adopt this new paradigm. Instead of focusing exclusively on maximizing its profits, this company is also concerned with reducing its carbon footprint. It invests in renewable energy, optimizes its processes to be more efficient and less polluting, and adopts recycling practices throughout its supply chain. By doing this, the company not only contributes to the global fight against climate change, but also positions itself as a leader in sustainability, which can attract conscious and loyal customers who value these initiatives. In this case, success is not only reflected in your financial statements, but also in improving the environment and strengthening your reputation.

But the new paradigm of success does not stop at the environment; It also extends to social responsibility. A truly successful company in the 21st century is one that cares about the well-being of its employees. This means offering fair wages, providing a safe and healthy work environment, and encouraging diversity and inclusion at all levels of the organization. A company that treats its workers well not only improves the quality of life of its employees, but also experiences greater talent retention, higher productivity, and a more positive work environment. These factors, in turn, contribute to long-term financial success.

In addition, the new paradigm of success also implies being a good neighbor in the communities where a company operates. Instead of recklessly exploiting local resources, a responsible company invests in communities, creates jobs, supports local initiatives and actively engages in solving social problems. This approach not only improves the lives of people in these communities, but also generates goodwill and strengthens the relationship between the company and its environment. When a company is seen as an ally, rather than an exploiter, its reputation rises, which can translate into greater business opportunities and more sustainable growth.

It is evident that this new paradigm is not just impractical idealism. More and more companies are demonstrating that it is possible to achieve significant financial success while acting responsibly. Large corporations like Patagonia, which has been an advocate for sustainability since its founding, show that it is possible to be profitable while fighting for the environment. Or companies like Ben & Jerry's, which have integrated social justice into their business model, demonstrating that companies can be forces for good in the world.

Ultimately, the new paradigm of success invites us to reconsider our priorities. It reminds us that companies do not exist in a vacuum, but are part of a social and environmental fabric that cannot be ignored. Instead of blindly pursuing profits at any cost, this new approach calls us to seek a more balanced success, one that considers the full impact of our actions and recognizes that true business success is measured not just by how much a company makes. , but also for what it contributes to the well-being of the world.

This shift in mindset can be difficult for some to adopt, especially those who have spent their entire career believing that the sole purpose of a business is to make a profit. However, it is a necessary change. As we face global challenges such as climate change, social inequality and resource scarcity, businesses have a crucial role to play in creating a more sustainable and equitable future. And those who adapt to this new paradigm of success will not only be on the right side of history, but will also be better positioned to thrive in the changing world of business.

Corporate Social Responsibility

Corporate Social Responsibility, or CSR, is a concept that has been gaining ground in the business world, especially in recent decades. But despite its growing popularity, there remains a lot of confusion about what it really means and, more importantly, why it is so crucial for businesses today. In simple terms, CSR is the commitment that companies make to operate ethically and contribute to economic development, while improving the quality of life of their employees, local communities and society in general. This commitment is not just a matter of complying with laws and regulations; is a business philosophy that goes beyond simple compliance to take a proactive stance in creating a positive impact on the world.

For many years, the prevailing idea was that companies only existed to generate profits for their shareholders. However, as societies have evolved, so have expectations about the role of business in the world. Today, companies are expected to be more than just engines of economic growth; They are expected to be responsible actors who actively contribute to social and environmental well-being.

This change in perception has not just been a matter of fashion or public relations. It is a reflection of the growing awareness that companies, because of their size, resources and influence, have the power and responsibility to make a significant difference in the world.

Implementing an effective CSR policy is not only an act of goodwill, but also a smart business strategy. Companies that commit to social responsibility often find that it brings them tangible benefits. One of the most obvious benefits is improved reputation. In a world where consumers are increasingly aware of business practices, companies that strive to do good often earn the loyalty and respect of their customers. This loyalty can translate into repeat sales, referrals, and a larger, more engaged customer base.

Additionally, CSR can be a key factor in attracting and retaining talent. Employees, especially younger ones, are increasingly looking to work for companies that align with their personal values. They want to feel proud of their employer and know that they are contributing to something bigger than themselves. Companies that demonstrate a strong commitment to social responsibility often find that they have a competitive advantage in attracting top talent and keeping their employees motivated and engaged.

Another crucial aspect of CSR is its impact on the long-term sustainability of a company. By making decisions that consider social and environmental impact, companies can avoid risks that could damage their reputation or economic viability in the future. For example, a company that manages its resources responsibly and reduces its environmental footprint not only contributes to the preservation of the planet, but can also reduce operating costs and protect itself against stricter environmental regulations that could be imposed in the future.

CSR can also open new business opportunities. In many cases, companies that commit to responsible practices discover emerging markets for sustainable products and services. For example, the growing demand for organic or fair trade products is evidence that consumers are willing to support companies that act ethically. By responding to these demands, companies can not only increase their revenue, but also differentiate themselves from the competition and strengthen their position in the market.

However, for CSR to be truly effective, it must be more than just a marketing strategy or a superficial compliance exercise. It must be deeply rooted in the company's culture and values. This means that all decisions, from the selection of suppliers to the way employees are treated, must reflect this commitment to social responsibility. It also means that CSR cannot be seen as a burden or an additional cost, but as an investment in the future of the company and in the well-being of all its stakeholders.

A clear example of how CSR can be transformed into a competitive advantage is the case of companies that are committed to fair trade. These companies ensure that producers in developing countries receive a fair price for their products, that they work in safe conditions, and that no child or forced labor is used in their supply chains. This commitment not only improves the lives of workers in these countries, but also builds trust and loyalty among consumers who want to support fair and ethical business practices.

Furthermore, CSR can be a powerful tool to address some of the most pressing challenges of our time, such as economic inequality and climate change. Companies have the resources and capacity to contribute significantly to solving these problems. For example, they can implement policies to reduce carbon emissions, invest in clean technologies, support education and development in disadvantaged communities, or promote diversity and inclusion in the workplace. By doing so, they are not only helping to create a better world, but they are also building a more stable and sustainable environment for their own businesses.

In short, Corporate Social Responsibility is neither a passing fad nor an obligation imposed from outside. It is a way of doing business that recognizes the interconnection between companies, society and the environment. It is a philosophy that understands that the long-term success of a company is intrinsically linked to the well-being of people and the planet. Embracing CSR does not mean giving up profits; It means redefining what it means to win. It means understanding that businesses can be powerful forces for good, and by doing so, they can create longer-lasting, more meaningful, and more complete success.

Companies that ignore CSR risk being left behind in a world that increasingly values ethics, sustainability and responsibility. But those who embrace it, not just as a policy, but as a fundamental part of their identity, will be better prepared to meet the challenges of the future and to thrive in an ever-changing world. In the end, Corporate Social Responsibility is not just good for society; It's good for business.

Evelyn Wright

The Impact of Climate Change on Companies

Climate change is one of the biggest and most urgent challenges facing our world today. Its effects are increasingly visible and, as the planet continues to warm, the consequences for humanity are profound and far-reaching. However, what is sometimes not discussed enough is how this phenomenon affects companies, both in the present and in the future. The impact of climate change on businesses is real, tangible and something that can no longer be ignored. It is not just an environmental problem; It's a business problem.

For starters, climate change is profoundly altering the environment in which businesses operate. Extreme weather events, such as hurricanes, floods, droughts and wildfires, are occurring with greater frequency and intensity. These events not only cause physical damage to business infrastructure, but also disrupt supply chains, reduce the availability of raw materials, and impact production and distribution. For example, a severe drought can devastate agriculture, which in turn impacts the food and beverage industries. Similarly, a violent storm can shut down factories, ports, and transportation routes, affecting businesses that depend on a steady supply of goods and services.

Additionally, climate change is altering the availability of key resources. Water, which is essential for almost all economic activities, is becoming increasingly scarce in many parts of the world due to rising temperatures and changes in precipitation patterns. Companies that depend on large amounts of water for their production, such as textile factories or power plants, are facing increasing challenges in securing the supply of this vital resource. This shortage not only increases operating costs, but can also lead to conflicts over water use between different sectors and communities, which in turn can damage the reputation of the companies involved.

Another important consequence of climate change is the increase in insurance costs. As extreme weather events become more frequent, insurers are reviewing their policies and increasing premiums to cover the associated risks. This means that companies have to pay more to protect their assets and operations, which directly affects their profit margins. In some cases, the risks may be so high that certain locations or activities become uninsurable, forcing companies to reconsider where and how they operate.

Climate change is also affecting demand for products and services. Consumers are increasingly aware of environmental issues and are changing their consumption habits accordingly. This is reflected in increased demand for sustainable products, such as organic food, electric vehicles and clothing made from recycled materials. Companies that do not adapt to these new market preferences may lose share and relevance compared to competitors that do. Additionally, governments around the world are implementing stricter regulations to reduce greenhouse gas emissions, directly affecting industries such as energy, transportation, and manufacturing. Companies that do not comply with these regulations face fines, restrictions and, in some cases, the inability to operate in certain markets.

The impact of climate change on businesses is not limited to costs and risks; It also presents opportunities for those willing to innovate and adapt. As demand for sustainable solutions increases, companies developing clean technologies, renewable energy or green products will be well positioned to capitalize on this change. For example, the solar energy industry has seen exponential growth in recent decades, driven by the need to reduce dependence on fossil fuels. Similarly, companies that adopt circular economy practices, such as recycling or reusing materials, can reduce costs and create new revenue streams.

However, to take advantage of these opportunities, companies must take a proactive approach to climate change. This means not only complying with current regulations, but going above and beyond to anticipate future regulations and market changes. Companies should regularly assess their carbon footprint and take steps to reduce it, whether by adopting renewable energy, improving energy efficiency or restructuring their supply chains. They must also be prepared to manage the risks associated with climate change, such as resource scarcity or extreme weather events, by diversifying suppliers and creating contingency plans.

Additionally, companies must consider the impact of climate change on their relationships with stakeholders. Investors, employees and consumers are paying increasing attention to how companies manage environmental and social risks. Companies that demonstrate a genuine commitment to sustainability will not only appeal to these stakeholders, but will also strengthen their reputation and brand in the process. On the other hand, those who ignore these issues run the risk of being perceived as irresponsible or disconnected from reality, which can damage their image and position in the market.

Ultimately, climate change is not an issue that companies can afford to ignore. Its effects are here, and will continue to intensify in the coming years. Companies that understand this and prepare to meet the challenges and seize the opportunities it presents will be better positioned to thrive in an ever-changing world. But more than that, they will have the opportunity to be part of the solution to one of the most critical problems of our time. They will be companies that not only seek economic benefit, but also care about the well-being of the planet and future generations.

The impact of climate change on businesses is profound and multifaceted, and companies' responses to this challenge will largely determine their success or failure in the future. Those that adapt, innovate and lead change will be better equipped to face the uncertainties of tomorrow. And in a world where climate change is reshaping the global economy, being resilient and responsible is no longer an option; It is a necessity.

The Real Cost of Indifference

Indifference, in any context, can seem like an easy and inconsequential option. It is the path of doing nothing, of looking the other way, of ignoring problems and hoping that they disappear on their own. However, in the business world, indifference has a real cost, a cost that can be devastating both for companies and for society as a whole. This cost is not always immediate or visible, but it accumulates over time and eventually takes a toll that few are prepared to pay.

When we talk about indifference in the business context, we refer to the lack of action against the social and environmental problems that surround a company. It is when companies decide that these problems are not their concern, that it does not affect them directly, or that it is not their place to take action. It's the "it's not my problem" attitude, a mentality that, while understandable from a short-term perspective, is deeply short-sighted and detrimental in the long term.

The first cost of indifference is the deterioration of reputation. In today's interconnected world, a company's actions or inactions are under constant scrutiny by consumers, the media, and society at large. A company that is indifferent to environmental problems, such as pollution or climate change, or social problems, such as labor exploitation or inequality, risks being seen as irresponsible or insensitive. This negative perception can alienate customers, decrease brand loyalty, and ultimately affect sales. In a competitive market, where consumer options are abundant, reputation is an invaluable asset that no company can afford to lose.

But loss of reputation is not the only cost of indifference. There are also the legal and regulatory costs. As social and environmental concerns become more pressing, governments and international bodies are introducing stricter regulations to address these issues. Companies that ignore these issues can find themselves on the wrong side of the law, facing fines, penalties and restrictions that can be very costly. Additionally, regulations are becoming more stringent, meaning that companies that do not adapt quickly to new realities will be forced to do so under pressure, at much higher costs than if they had taken proactive measures from the beginning.

Another significant cost of indifference is the loss of opportunities. While some companies choose to ignore problems, others see them as opportunities to innovate, differentiate and lead. For example, as demand for sustainable and ethical products grows, companies that anticipate this trend and adapt their business models can capitalize on these new markets. Indifferent companies, on the other hand, not only miss these opportunities, but are also left behind in a rapidly evolving market. By not adapting, they become less competitive and ultimately risk becoming obsolete.

Furthermore, indifference also affects companies internally. Employees, especially younger ones, are looking to work for companies that share their values and care about more than just profits. A company that shows indifference to social and environmental issues may have difficulty attracting and retaining talent. Employees who do not feel aligned with their employer's values can become demotivated, which affects their productivity and engagement. This, in turn, can lead to high staff turnover, which involves additional costs in terms of recruitment, training and loss of knowledge and experience.

The negative impact of indifference also extends to society at large. When companies do not assume their responsibility in issues such as social justice, equal opportunities, or environmental sustainability, they leave a void that other actors, such as governments or non-governmental organizations, have to fill. This can lead to increased regulation, taxes and controls which, although necessary, may be less efficient and more costly for businesses and society as a whole. Furthermore, by not actively contributing to solving these problems, companies miss the opportunity to improve people's living conditions and build an environment in which they and their communities can thrive.

Finally, the real cost of indifference manifests itself in vulnerability to long-term risks. Ignored problems do not disappear; They just get worse. Climate change, social inequality, resource scarcity, all these problems have a cumulative impact that, over time, can threaten the viability of companies that are not prepared to face them. Companies that do not take these risks into account in their strategic planning are in a dangerous position. Indifference today can mean a crisis tomorrow, and for many companies, the cost of not being prepared for that crisis can be the difference between survival and failure.

In short, indifference is not a costless option; It is a decision that has serious and lasting repercussions. From loss of reputation and opportunities, to increased legal costs, erosion of employee morale and exposure to long-term risks, the effects of indifference are felt in all aspects of a company. And beyond the immediate impacts on the company itself, indifference contributes to perpetuating social and environmental problems that affect the entire society. In a world increasingly aware of these problems, indifference is not only irresponsible, but also unsustainable.

It is vital that businesses understand that action, not indifference, is what is required to thrive in today's world. By facing problems head-on, taking responsibility and actively seeking solutions, companies not only protect their own interests, but also contribute to creating a fairer, more sustainable and more prosperous world for all. Ignoring problems may seem like an easier option, but in the long term, the real cost of indifference is much greater than that of acting. And in a global environment where challenges are increasingly complex and urgent, companies cannot afford to be indifferent.

Green Innovation

Green innovation is a concept that has gained importance in recent decades, as the world has begun to recognize the urgency of addressing the environmental challenges we face. In simple terms, green innovation refers to the creation of new products, services and processes that are not only profitable, but are also sustainable and environmentally friendly. Unlike traditional innovation, which often focuses exclusively on efficiency and cost reduction, green innovation aims to minimize the negative impact on the planet while generating economic and social benefits.

The concept of green innovation arises from the need to find solutions to the environmental problems that we have created over the years, from air and water pollution, to the loss of biodiversity and climate change. These issues are not only challenges for humanity as a whole, but also pose significant risks for businesses. Those that ignore the need to adopt sustainable practices expose themselves to stricter regulations, loss of reputation and decreased customer loyalty. On the other hand, companies that invest in green innovation not only contribute to the solution of these problems, but also position themselves as leaders in a market that increasingly values sustainability.

A clear example of green innovation is the development of renewable energies, such as solar and wind. As fossil fuels become depleted and their harmful effects on the environment become more evident, the need to find clean and sustainable energy sources has become paramount. Companies around the world have responded to this need by investing in technology to harness energy from the sun and wind. These energies are not only infinite, but they are also much less harmful to the environment than fossil fuels. By adopting these technologies, companies not only reduce their carbon footprint, but also protect themselves against fluctuations in oil and gas prices, allowing them to operate more stable and predictable in the long term.

Another example of green innovation is the circular economy. Traditionally, the economy has operated on a linear "take, make, throw away" model, in which resources are extracted, goods are produced, and eventually disposed of as garbage. This model has led to unsustainable consumption of resources and a massive accumulation of waste that damages the environment. The circular economy proposes a radical change in this way of thinking, by seeking to keep products, materials and resources in use for as long as possible. This is achieved through recycling, reuse and repair, rather than simply disposing of products at the end of their useful life. Companies that adopt this approach not only reduce their environmental impact, but also discover new business opportunities, such as creating products from recycled materials or offering repair and maintenance services.

In addition to renewable energy and the circular economy, green innovation also manifests itself in the development of new materials that are more sustainable. For example, in the textile industry, some companies are investing in the development of fabrics made from recycled materials, such as plastic bottles, or from natural fibers that require less water and pesticides to grow. These materials are not only less harmful to the environment, but can also be of higher quality and durability, adding value for consumers. Similarly, in the packaging industry, companies are looking for alternatives to plastic, such as biodegradable or reusable packaging, which help reduce the amount of waste that ends up in landfills or the oceans.

Green innovation is not limited to tangible products; It also applies to processes and the way companies operate. For example, some companies are adopting energy efficiency practices in their operations, such as installing LED lighting systems, optimizing production processes to reduce energy consumption, or using energy management technologies that monitor and optimize the use of resources in real time. These practices not only reduce the environmental impact of the company's operations, but can also result in significant savings in operating costs. In fact, many times, investing in green technologies quickly pays for itself thanks to reduced energy consumption and utility bills.

However, green innovation is not just a matter of technology or process changes. It also implies a change in mentality, both in companies and in consumers. Companies that are truly committed to green innovation understand that sustainability is not an accessory or a fad, but a fundamental element of their business strategy. These companies are willing to question traditional approaches, invest in research and development, and collaborate with other actors, such as governments, universities and non-governmental organizations, to find innovative solutions to environmental challenges. This approach not only allows them to stay at the forefront of innovation, but also helps them build stronger, longer-lasting relationships with their customers and other stakeholders.

On the other hand, consumers also play a crucial role in promoting green innovation. As more people become aware of the environmental impacts of their consumer choices, demand for sustainable products and services continues to grow. Companies that can meet this demand are in a prime position to capture new markets and strengthen their brand. Additionally, by educating consumers about the importance of sustainability and offering greener options, companies can contribute to a broader cultural shift toward more responsible consumption.

However, for all the potential benefits of green innovation, there are also challenges that must be overcome. One of the main challenges is the initial cost of investing in sustainable technologies and processes. Although these costs are often recovered over time, the initial investment can be significant, which can deter some companies, especially small and medium-sized ones, from adopting green practices. To overcome this obstacle, it is important for companies to see green innovation not as a cost, but as an investment in their future. Additionally, governments and other institutions can play an important role by providing incentives, such as subsidies or tax credits, to help companies transition to more sustainable practices.

Another challenge is the need to change business mindset and culture. In many companies, especially those that have long operated under traditional models, there may be resistance to change. Implementing green innovation requires commitment at the leadership level and clear communication of the benefits at all levels of the organization. It is also important to involve employees in the process, as their participation and support are essential to the success of any sustainability initiative.

In conclusion, green innovation is more than a trend; It is a necessity in a world where resources are limited and environmental challenges are increasingly urgent. Companies that embrace green innovation not only contribute to the preservation of the environment, but also position themselves to succeed in an evolving market. Whether through the development of new technologies, the adoption of sustainable practices or the creation of products and services that respond to the needs of conscious consumers, green innovation offers a path to a more prosperous and sustainable future for all. And while the challenges are real, the opportunities that green innovation offers are enormous for those companies that are willing to lead the change.

Circular Economy

The circular economy is a concept that is transforming the way we think about production and consumption. Unlike the traditional economic model, which is based on the idea of "take, make and throw away", the circular economy proposes a much more sustainable and efficient approach, in which resources are used more intelligently and waste is minimized. . This model is inspired by natural cycles, where the concept of garbage does not exist, but everything has a purpose and a place in the life cycle. In other words, the circular economy seeks to close the resource cycle, ensuring that materials remain in use for as long as possible and are recycled or reused at the end of their useful life.

The traditional economic model, also known as linear economics, has been the norm for centuries. In this system, natural resources are extracted from the environment, transformed into products through manufacturing processes, consumed, and finally disposed of. This approach has enabled large-scale industrial and economic development, but has also led to unsustainable exploitation of natural resources, massive waste generation and environmental degradation. Over time, it has become clear that this model is not viable in the long term, especially in a world with finite resources and a growing population.

This is where the circular economy comes in. Instead of following a linear trajectory from start to finish, the circular economy proposes a continuous cycle, where products and materials are reused, recycled or revalued, instead of being thrown away. This approach not only reduces pressure on natural resources, but also decreases the amount of waste that ends up in landfills or polluting the environment. The circular economy, therefore, is not only a solution to environmental problems, but also an opportunity for companies to innovate, save costs and create long-term value.

One of the fundamental principles of the circular economy is design for durability, repair and recyclability. This means that, from the moment a product is conceived, its entire life cycle is taken into account. Designers must think about how the product will be manufactured, how it will be used, how it will be repaired if damaged, and how it will break down at the end of its useful life. For example, instead of creating products that are thrown away after a single use, companies can design products that are easy to disassemble and repair, or that are made from recyclable materials that can be reused in new products.

A clear example of this approach is the fashion industry, where the "fast fashion" model has been dominant for many years. This model is based on the quick and cheap production of clothing that is worn for a short time and then thrown away. However, this approach has led to enormous waste of resources and environmental pollution. In response, some fashion brands are embracing the circular economy by designing clothing that lasts longer, can be easily repaired, or is made from recycled materials. In addition, they are exploring business models that encourage resale, rental or recycling of garments at the end of their useful life.

Another example of a circular economy is found in the electronics industry. Electronic devices, such as mobile phones and computers, are notoriously difficult to recycle due to the complexity of their components and the variety of materials used. However, some companies are taking a circular approach by designing modular devices that can be easily disassembled and repaired, or by offering buyback programs where old devices are collected and recycled. This approach not only reduces electronic waste, but also allows companies to recover valuable materials that can be reused in the manufacture of new devices.

The circular economy also has a significant impact on waste management. Instead of seeing waste as a problem, the circular economy sees it as an opportunity. For example, organic waste, such as food scraps, can be composted and returned to the soil as fertilizer, instead of being sent to a landfill where it will generate methane, a potent greenhouse gas. Similarly, industrial waste, such as manufacturing byproducts, can be reused or recycled instead of being thrown away. This approach not only reduces the amount of waste generated, but also creates new business opportunities for companies that can transform waste into valuable resources.

Furthermore, the circular economy promotes efficiency in the use of resources. This means that companies look for ways to use fewer resources to produce more, and to maximize the value of resources already in use. For example, instead of extracting new raw materials, companies can recycle existing materials, thereby reducing demand for natural resources. Not only does this have environmental benefits, but it can also result in significant savings in production costs. By reducing dependence on natural resources, companies also protect themselves against volatility in raw material prices and potential supply chain disruptions.

However, the transition to a circular economy is not easy and presents several challenges. One of the main obstacles is the change in mentality that is required in both companies and consumers. For a long time, we have been accustomed to a consumption model based on abundance and planned obsolescence, where products are designed to be replaced frequently. Changing this mindset requires education, both in business and in society, so that we understand the value of durability, repair and reuse. Companies must be willing to invest in research and development to design products that conform to the principles of the circular economy, and consumers must be willing to support these initiatives by purchasing sustainable products and adopting more responsible consumption habits.

Another challenge is the infrastructure needed to support a circular economy. So that materials can be recycled and reused efficiently, adequate infrastructure is needed for the collection, classification and processing of waste. This may require significant investment by governments and businesses, as well as collaboration between different sectors and regions. Furthermore, the circular economy requires a regulatory framework that encourages sustainability and penalizes waste. This may include tax incentives for companies that adopt circular practices, regulations that promote recycling and reuse, and policies that encourage innovation in sustainable materials and processes.

Despite these challenges, the potential benefits of the circular economy are enormous. For companies, the circular economy offers the opportunity to reduce costs, increase efficiency, and open new markets. By designing products that are durable, repairable and recyclable, companies can improve their competitiveness and resilience in an ever-changing global market. Additionally, by adopting a circular approach, companies can improve their reputation and strengthen their relationship with consumers, who increasingly value sustainability.

For society as a whole, the circular economy can contribute to job creation and sustainable economic development. By encouraging repair, recycling and reuse, new jobs can be created in sectors such as waste management, manufacturing of recycled products, and the repair and maintenance of durable goods. Additionally, the circular economy can help reduce pressure on natural resources, which is essential for the long-term sustainability of our planet.

In short, the circular economy is an innovative and necessary approach to confront the environmental and economic challenges of our time. By breaking away from the traditional "take, make, waste" model and adopting a more sustainable and efficient approach, the circular economy offers a roadmap to a more prosperous and equitable future. Although the transition will not be easy, the potential benefits are enormous, both for companies and for society as a whole. By closing the resource loop and maximizing the value of materials, the circular economy not only helps us protect the environment, but also offers us new opportunities to innovate, grow and prosper.

Renewable Energy and Energy Efficiency in Business

The transition to renewable energy and energy efficiency is one of the most significant and necessary changes any business can undertake today. In a world where natural resources are finite and climate change is a real and present threat, companies have a responsibility to reexamine the way they consume energy and look for more sustainable ways of operating. This change is not only beneficial for the environment, but also offers long-term competitive advantages, reducing operating costs and improving the company's reputation among consumers and other stakeholders.

Renewable energy refers to energy sources that are regenerated naturally and continuously. Unlike fossil fuels, such as oil, natural gas, and coal, which are extracted from the earth and depleted over time, renewable energy, such as solar, wind, hydroelectric, and geothermal, comes from resources that are available indefinitely. By adopting renewable energy, companies not only contribute to the reduction of greenhouse gas emissions, but also protect themselves from the volatility of fossil fuel prices and potential supply chain disruptions.

Solar energy is perhaps the most accessible and widely adopted renewable energy source today. With advances in solar panel technology, it is possible to capture the sun's energy more efficiently and at an increasingly lower cost. Companies of all sizes are installing solar panels on the roofs of their buildings or on available land, generating their own electricity and reducing their dependence on the electrical grid. This initial investment in solar energy may seem significant, but in the long term, the electricity cost savings can be substantial, especially as energy prices continue to rise. Additionally, in many places, governments offer tax incentives and subsidies for companies that invest in solar energy, which can help pay for the investment more quickly.

Wind energy is another renewable energy source that has gained popularity in recent decades. Wind turbines, which convert wind energy into electricity, are a viable option for companies that have access to areas with good wind resources. Although installing wind turbines requires a considerable initial investment, the long-term benefits are similar to those of solar energy: a reduction in electricity costs and greater energy independence. Additionally, wind energy is one of the cleanest energy sources available, as it produces no emissions or waste during operation.

Hydroelectric and geothermal are two other renewable energy sources that, although less common than solar and wind, also offer important benefits. Hydropower, which harnesses the power of moving water to generate electricity, is a reliable and stable source of energy. Geothermal energy, meanwhile, uses the earth's natural heat to generate electricity or to provide heating and cooling. These energy sources are especially useful in regions where natural resources allow it, and their adoption can help diversify a company's energy matrix, further reducing its dependence on fossil fuels.

But the adoption of renewable energy is only part of the equation. Energy efficiency, that is, using the energy we consume more intelligently and effectively, is equally crucial. Being energy efficient means using less energy to do the same amount of work, or even more. This not only reduces operating costs, but also decreases the company's carbon footprint, which is essential in a world facing climate change.

A simple example of energy efficiency is LED lighting. Unlike traditional incandescent bulbs, which waste much of the energy as heat, LED lights convert most of the energy into light, making them much more efficient. Additionally, LED bulbs have a much longer lifespan, reducing the need for frequent replacements and therefore the waste generated. Switching to LED lighting in an office, factory or store can result in significant savings on electricity bills, and is one of the easiest and most effective ways to improve energy efficiency.

Another example is the optimization of heating, ventilation and air conditioning (HVAC) systems. These systems are responsible for a large portion of any building's energy consumption, and improving them can have a big impact on overall energy efficiency. Businesses can install programmable or smart thermostats that automatically adjust the temperature based on the time of day or building occupancy, preventing wasted energy. Additionally, performing regular maintenance and upgrading outdated equipment can ensure that your HVAC system is operating optimally and consuming the least amount of energy possible.

Energy audits are another valuable tool to improve energy efficiency in the business. These audits involve a thorough assessment of a company's energy use, identifying areas where consumption can be reduced and efficiency improved. Once these areas are identified, companies can implement specific solutions, such as modernizing equipment, improving insulation in buildings, or implementing more efficient operating practices. In the end, energy audits not only help reduce energy costs, but also provide a clear roadmap for long-term sustainability.

In addition to the financial and environmental benefits, the transition to renewable energy and improving energy efficiency also have a positive impact on the company's reputation. In a world where consumers are increasingly aware of environmental issues, companies that demonstrate a genuine commitment to sustainability are viewed more favorably. This can translate into greater customer loyalty, a better relationship with investors, and a greater ability to attract and retain talent. New generations of workers look for employers who share their values, and a company that invests in renewable energy and energy efficiency demonstrates a commitment to the future of the planet and social responsibility.

Additionally, the focus on renewable energy and energy efficiency can open up new business opportunities. For example, some companies are finding ways to monetize their renewable energy investments by selling the excess electricity they generate back to the power grid, or by developing new products and services related to sustainability. Companies that lead the adoption of these technologies can also position themselves as thought leaders in their industries, influencing energy policy and sustainability practices within their sector.

However, the transition to renewable energy and improving energy efficiency is not without challenges. One of the main obstacles is the initial cost of investing in new technologies. Although renewable energy prices have decreased significantly in recent years, the installation of solar panels, wind turbines or energy efficiency systems can still represent a considerable expense, especially for small and medium-sized businesses. To overcome this challenge, companies must view these investments not as an expense, but as an investment in their future. Additionally, government incentives, green financing programs, and partnerships with other companies or institutions can help reduce costs and ease the transition.

Another challenge is resistance to change. Companies that have long operated under a traditional model may be reluctant to adopt new technologies or practices, especially if they are unfamiliar with them. Overcoming this resistance requires a strong commitment from company leadership, as well as employee education and training to ensure everyone understands the benefits of renewable energy and energy efficiency. Additionally, it is important for companies to stay informed about the latest trends and developments in the energy field, so that they can make informed decisions and adapt to an ever-changing environment.

In short, transitioning to renewable energy and improving energy efficiency are essential steps for any company that wants to be competitive and sustainable in the future. Not only do they allow companies to reduce their operating costs and minimize their environmental impact, but they also improve their reputation, open new business opportunities and prepare them to face the challenges of the 21st century. Although the transition may present challenges, the long-term benefits far outweigh the initial costs. By adopting renewable energy and improving energy efficiency, companies are not only investing in their own success, but also in the future of the planet and the well-being of generations to come.

Responsible Supply

Responsible sourcing is a business approach that seeks to ensure that all products and services a company purchases and uses come from sources that respect both the environment and human rights. Instead of focusing solely on getting the best prices or fastest delivery, responsible sourcing considers a number of broader factors, such as the working conditions of workers in the supply chain, the environmental impact of production processes, and the sustainability of the resources used. This approach is not only ethically correct, but also makes sense from a business perspective, as a sustainable and fair supply chain can strengthen a company's reputation, reduce risks and ensure stable supply in the long term.

Traditionally, many companies have looked for suppliers who can offer products and materials at the lowest possible cost, regardless of how they are produced or the conditions under which those suppliers' employees work. This approach, although it may reduce costs in the short term, carries a number of significant risks. For example, if a supplier is involved in abusive labor practices or unsustainable exploitation of natural resources, this can seriously damage the reputation of the purchasing company if these practices come to light. Additionally, supply chain disruptions, whether due to labor disputes, environmental disasters, or regulatory issues, can severely impact a company's operations. A responsible sourcing approach helps mitigate these risks by ensuring that suppliers meet certain ethical and sustainability standards.

A key component of responsible sourcing is selecting suppliers that align with the company's values and goals. This means that, instead of simply looking for the cheapest supplier, companies must evaluate their potential partners based on criteria such as respect for labor rights, compliance with environmental standards, and transparency in their operations. This may require conducting audits, implementing codes of conduct for suppliers, and working closely with suppliers to ensure they meet expectations. By working with suppliers who share their values, companies can not only ensure they are supporting ethical practices, but can also foster long-term relationships based on trust and collaboration.

Another important aspect of responsible sourcing is traceability, which involves the ability to track products and materials throughout the entire supply chain, from their origin to their final destination. Traceability allows companies to ensure that the materials they use come from responsible sources and are not contributing to problems such as deforestation, labor exploitation or pollution. In industries such as food, fashion or electronics, traceability is especially crucial, as consumers are increasingly aware of the impacts of their purchases and demand transparency about the origin of the products they buy.

For example, in the food industry, responsible sourcing may involve ensuring that agricultural products are grown sustainably, without the excessive use of pesticides or fertilizers that can harm the environment. It can also mean ensuring that workers on farms and processing plants are paid fairly and work in safe conditions. In the fashion industry, responsible sourcing could include ensuring that garments are not produced in factories with unsafe working conditions or sweatshops, and that the materials used, such as cotton or leather, are sourced in ways that do not contribute to environmental degradation.

In the technology sector, responsible sourcing is equally critical. The production of electronic devices often involves the extraction of minerals such as cobalt and tin, which can come from conflict regions or from mines that do not meet environmental and labor standards. Responsible technology companies work to ensure that the minerals they use come from sources that respect human rights and do not finance armed conflicts. This may require implementing traceability systems and collaborating with international organizations to ensure materials are sourced ethically.

Responsible sourcing is not just about avoiding harm, but also about creating positive value. Companies that take this approach often look for opportunities to improve conditions in the communities where their products come from. This could include investing in community projects, supporting education and health initiatives, or working with suppliers to improve their labor and environmental practices. By doing so, companies not only improve the sustainability of their own operations, but also contribute to the sustainable development of the communities in which they operate.

Furthermore, responsible sourcing can also be a key factor in innovation. By looking for materials and processes that are more sustainable, companies often discover new ways to improve their products, reduce costs and differentiate themselves in the market. For example, a fashion company looking for sustainable alternatives to conventional cotton could discover new materials, such as organic cotton or recycled fibers, that are not only better for the environment, but also offer new design and marketing opportunities. Similarly, a technology company that commits to using only ethically sourced minerals could develop new manufacturing processes that not only meet ethical standards, but are also more efficient and profitable.

Implementing a responsible sourcing program can be challenging, especially for smaller companies that may not have the resources to conduct extensive audits or develop complex traceability systems. However, there are steps all companies can take to move towards more responsible sourcing. These steps may include creating a code of conduct for suppliers, conducting risk assessments to identify areas of greatest concern in the supply chain, and collaborating with other companies, non-governmental organizations, and governments to share best practices. and develop common solutions.

In some cases, companies may face difficult dilemmas when implementing responsible sourcing. For example, a long-standing supplier that offers good prices and high-quality products might not meet the company's ethical or sustainability standards. In these cases, it is important for companies to be transparent and work with their suppliers to improve their practices. This may involve providing technical or financial support to help the supplier meet standards, or ultimately seeking new suppliers that are more aligned with the company's values. The key is to maintain a long-term focus, recognizing that responsible sourcing is a continuous process of improvement and collaboration.

Ultimately, responsible sourcing is essential for any company that wants to be sustainable and competitive in the 21st century. In a world where consumers and other stakeholders increasingly demand transparency and accountability, companies that do not align with these values risk being left behind. On the other hand, companies that adopt a responsible sourcing approach can not only reduce risks and improve their reputation, but also discover new business opportunities and strengthen their relationships with suppliers and customers. In the end, responsible sourcing is not just a matter of doing the right thing, but also doing what is best for the business in the long term.

Business and Human Rights

Companies, in their search for success and profitability, have a fundamental responsibility that goes beyond their products or services: respect and promote human rights. This commitment is not optional nor something that should be considered a mere formality; It is an ethical and legal obligation that must be at the heart of all business operations. Respect for human rights encompasses all dimensions of business activities, from how employees are treated to how they interact with local communities, suppliers and customers. This approach is not only essential for people's well-being, but is also key to the long-term sustainability of any business.

When we talk about human rights in the business context, we refer to a series of principles that protect the dignity and equality of all people. These rights include, among others, the right to fair working conditions, the right to health and safety, the prohibition of child labor and exploitation, protection against discrimination, and the right to a fair wage. Companies, as influential actors in society, have the power to positively or negatively impact these rights through their decisions and actions.

One of the most obvious aspects of the relationship between companies and human rights is the treatment that employees receive. Working conditions must be decent and safe, offering an environment where workers can carry out their tasks without fear of accidents, abuse or exploitation. This means that companies must comply with all local and international labor laws, but also go further, ensuring that their labor practices are fair and equitable. For example, employees must receive a salary that not only meets the legal minimum wage, but is also sufficient to cover the basic needs of themselves and their families. In addition, benefits such as access to healthcare and the possibility of professional development should be offered, which contributes to the overall well-being of employees.

Respect for human rights also extends to protection against discrimination in the workplace. Companies must ensure that all employees are treated equally, regardless of gender, race, religion, sexual orientation, disability or other personal characteristics.

This means not only having clear anti-discrimination policies, but also fostering an inclusive culture in which all employees feel valued and respected. Diversity in the workplace is not only a matter of fairness, but can also be a driver of innovation and creativity, as different perspectives and experiences can lead to new ideas and solutions.

Another critical aspect is the prevention of child and forced labor in the supply chain. Many companies, especially those that operate globally, rely on suppliers in countries where labor regulations may be less strict or where poverty leads to the exploitation of vulnerable workers. It is essential that companies take active steps to ensure that their products are not the result of child exploitation or forced labor. This may include conducting supplier audits, establishing codes of conduct that prohibit these practices, and collaborating with non-governmental organizations to improve working conditions in the communities where they operate.

The relationship between companies and human rights is not limited only to their employees and suppliers. It also includes the local communities where the companies operate. Companies have a duty to respect the rights of these communities, ensuring that their operations do not cause harm to health, the environment or social well-being. For example, a company that extracts natural resources must ensure that its activities do not pollute the water or air of nearby communities, and that they do not displace people from their lands without their consent and fair compensation. Companies must also involve communities in decisions that affect them, ensuring that their voices are heard and respected.

Additionally, companies have a responsibility to respect consumer rights. This involves being transparent about the products and services they offer, ensuring they are not misleading or harmful. For example, food companies must be clear about the ingredients and nutritional values of their products, and technology companies must protect the privacy of their users' data. Respecting consumer rights not only builds trust, but is also essential to maintaining long-term customer loyalty.

Implementing a human rights approach in business operations is not a simple task, especially for large, global companies that operate in multiple countries and cultural contexts. However, it is essential that companies seriously commit to this responsibility. This requires a combination of clear policies, robust internal processes, and a corporate culture that values and promotes respect for human rights at all levels of the organization.

Companies must also be prepared to face dilemmas and challenges in their commitment to human rights. For example, in some countries, local laws may conflict with international human rights standards. In these cases, companies must work to find solutions that respect human rights without violating local laws, which may require a delicate balance and, in some cases, dialogue with governments and other stakeholders to promote legislative changes.

It is important to highlight that the commitment to human rights should not be seen only as a burden or an obligation, but as an opportunity for companies. Companies that respect and promote human rights can improve their reputation, increase customer loyalty, attract and retain talent, and reduce legal and reputational risks. Furthermore, companies that lead in this area can positively influence their sectors and society in general, promoting a change towards a more just and equitable world.

In short, businesses have a crucial role in protecting and promoting human rights. This commitment must be comprehensive, covering all areas of business operation, from working conditions to the supply chain, the impact on local communities and consumer rights. Although this approach may present challenges, it also offers important long-term benefits, both for businesses and for society as a whole. In an increasingly connected and aware world, companies that take their human rights responsibilities seriously will be better positioned to thrive and contribute to a more sustainable and equitable future for all.

Evelyn Wright

Diversity and Inclusion

Diversity and inclusion in companies is an issue of increasing importance, not only for ethical reasons, but also because it has a direct impact on the success and sustainability of businesses. Diversity refers to the presence of people with different characteristics and backgrounds in an organization, such as gender, race, sexual orientation, age, physical and cognitive abilities, and cultural and social experiences. Inclusion, for its part, refers to creating an environment in which all these people feel valued, respected and empowered to contribute fully to the success of the company.

In a globalized and changing world, companies that do not recognize the importance of diversity and inclusion risk being left behind. Diverse organizations can draw on a broader range of perspectives and experiences, allowing them to innovate and solve problems more effectively. Additionally, when employees feel included and valued, they are more likely to be engaged in their work, leading to greater productivity and loyalty. Therefore, diversity and inclusion are not only right from a moral perspective, but are also essential for business competitiveness.

One of the most important aspects of diversity and inclusion is equal opportunity. This means that all people, regardless of their background or personal characteristics, should have the same opportunities to advance their career and contribute to the success of the company. To achieve this, companies must ensure that their hiring, promotion and career development processes are fair and transparent. This may involve reviewing and adjusting policies and practices to eliminate any conscious or unconscious biases that may be preventing some people from reaching their full potential.

For example, in the hiring process, companies should strive to attract candidates from diverse backgrounds and ensure that hiring decisions are based on skills and competencies, rather than stereotypes or biases. This could involve using diverse interview panels, reviewing job requirements to ensure they are not unnecessarily exclusionary, and implementing unconscious bias training programs for everyone involved in the selection process. Additionally, companies should consider implementing mentoring and career development programs that help people from underrepresented groups advance their careers.

Diversity and inclusion must also be reflected in the organizational culture. Creating an inclusive environment requires more than just formal policies; It also involves fostering an environment of respect, collaboration and mutual support. This means that everyone should feel safe expressing their opinions and being authentic in the workplace, without fear of discrimination or exclusion. To achieve this, business leaders must role model respect and inclusion, and must be willing to confront and address any behavior or attitude that is not aligned with these values.

Inclusive culture is also reinforced when companies celebrate and value differences. This could include organizing events that promote cross-cultural understanding, recognizing diverse cultural holidays and traditions, and adapting policies and practices to reflect the needs of a diverse workforce. For example, companies could offer flexible work options to accommodate family or religious responsibilities, or they could adapt their dress policies to allow for the expression of cultural or religious identity.

It is important to highlight that diversity and inclusion should not only be considered an internal company issue, but also as a responsibility towards society in general. Companies have the power and influence to promote diversity and inclusion in society through their hiring decisions, their relationships with suppliers, and their community involvement. For example, companies can support suppliers and business partners that promote diversity and inclusion, and can participate in community initiatives that promote equal opportunity and respect for diversity.

Additionally, companies can play a crucial role in championing diversity and inclusion in their industry and in society at large. This could include collaborating with other businesses, non-governmental organizations and governments to promote inclusive policies and practices, as well as participating in public campaigns that advocate for equality and respect for all people. By taking a leadership role in promoting diversity and inclusion, companies not only enhance their own reputation, but also contribute to building a more just and equitable society.

However, it is important to recognize that implementing diversity and inclusion in a company is not without challenges. Resistance to change, unconscious biases, and existing power dynamics can make it difficult to create a truly inclusive environment. Therefore, it is essential that companies commit to a continuous process of learning and improvement in this area. This may involve collecting and analyzing data on diversity in the company, conducting work environment surveys to assess inclusion, and implementing training and awareness programs for all employees.

Another crucial aspect is inclusive leadership. Company leaders should be the biggest advocates for diversity and inclusion, and they should be willing to challenge the status quo when necessary. This requires courage and vision, as well as the ability to listen and learn from the experiences of others. Inclusive leaders must also be able to build diverse teams and foster a culture of respect and collaboration, where all voices are heard and valued. Additionally, they must be accountable for their actions and decisions, and be willing to adjust their approach based on changing results and needs.

It is important to remember that diversity and inclusion are not overnight goals, but are an ongoing journey. Companies must be willing to regularly evaluate their progress, learn from their mistakes, and adapt their strategies as necessary. This process may require time and effort, but the long-term benefits are significant. A company that truly values diversity and inclusion will not only attract and retain top talent, but will also be more innovative, more agile, and better equipped to meet the challenges of the future.

In short, diversity and inclusion are not only essential to social justice, they are also critical to business success in today's world. By creating an environment where all people feel valued and respected, companies can harness the power of diversity to innovate, solve problems, and compete more effectively. Although there may be challenges along the way, a commitment to diversity and inclusion is an investment in the future of the company and the well-being of society as a whole. Companies that lead in this space will not only be better positioned to thrive in a changing world, but they will also be contributing to building a more just, equitable and inclusive world for all.

Empowering Local Communities

Empowering local communities is an essential concept for any company that aspires to have a positive and lasting impact on society. It is not just about carrying out charitable activities or fulfilling basic responsibilities, but about creating real and sustainable opportunities that benefit the people who live and work in the areas where the company operates. By empowering local communities, businesses not only contribute to social well-being, but also build stronger relationships, gain greater community support, and foster a more stable and prosperous environment, which is critical to their own long-term success.

The first step to empowering local communities is to understand their specific needs and challenges. Each community is unique, with its own culture, history and problems. Companies should take the time to get to know the people and circumstances around them, rather than assuming that a single solution will work in all contexts. This approach requires a genuine commitment to listening to community leaders, local organizations and residents themselves. Through open and honest dialogue, companies can identify areas where they can make a real difference, whether it is improving local infrastructure, supporting education, promoting health, or creating decent jobs.

Job creation is one of the most effective ways businesses can empower local communities. By offering well-paying, secure jobs, businesses not only provide income for workers, but also strengthen the overall local economy. Additionally, when companies hire locally, they are not only helping people earn a living, but they are also tapping into local experience and knowledge, which can be invaluable to the success of their operations. However, it is not just about creating jobs, but ensuring that those jobs are quality, with fair working conditions, training and development opportunities, and a respectful and inclusive work environment.

In addition to employment, businesses can empower local communities through supporting education and training. Education is a fundamental pillar for the development of any community, as it provides people with the skills and knowledge necessary to improve their lives and contribute to general well-being. Businesses can support education in a variety of ways, such as investing in local schools, offering scholarship programs for students, or providing technical and career training to local workers. These types of initiatives not only benefit people in the community, but also help companies develop a more qualified and engaged workforce.

Empowering local communities can also be achieved by promoting entrepreneurship and supporting small businesses. Small businesses are often the heart of local economies, providing vital jobs and services. Larger companies can support these small businesses in various ways, such as offering advice, training, and access to resources and markets. By helping small businesses grow and prosper, larger companies are not only strengthening the local economy, they are also creating a more diverse and resilient business ecosystem. This approach can include local purchasing programs, where companies commit to purchasing goods and services from local suppliers, thereby contributing to the economic growth of the community.

Environmental sustainability is another crucial aspect of community empowerment. Local communities often depend directly on their natural environment for their livelihoods, whether through agriculture, fishing, tourism, or other activities. Companies operating in these areas have a responsibility to ensure that their activities do not harm the local environment and, in fact, must look for ways to contribute to its preservation. This may include implementing sustainable business practices, such as reducing pollution, efficient use of natural resources, and restoring degraded habitats. By protecting the natural environment, companies are not only preserving the resource base of local communities, they are also ensuring the long-term sustainability of their own operations.

Empowering local communities also refers to creating an environment in which people have a voice and decision-making power over matters that affect their lives. Companies can encourage this type of participation through consultation and constant dialogue with communities, ensuring that their opinions and concerns are heard and taken into account in business decisions. This may include creating community advisory committees, holding regular meetings with local leaders, or implementing feedback mechanisms that allow residents to express their concerns and suggestions. By actively involving communities in the decision-making process, companies are not only building stronger, more trusting relationships, but they are also creating a sense of ownership and shared responsibility in projects and activities that affect the community.

A concrete example of how companies can empower local communities is through investment in infrastructure that benefits the community. This may include the construction or improvement of roads, bridges, drinking water systems, health facilities, and other essential services. These investments not only improve the quality of life for people in the community, but can also facilitate company operations by creating a more functional and efficient environment. It is important that these investments are made in consultation with the community to ensure that they truly meet their needs and priorities.

Empowering local communities also involves a commitment to equity and social justice. This means that companies must strive to ensure that the benefits of their activities are distributed fairly and equitably, and do not perpetuate or exacerbate existing inequalities. For example, companies must ensure that their operations do not displace indigenous or vulnerable communities, and must work to ensure that all community members have access to the opportunities and benefits generated by their activities. This also means supporting the fight against discrimination and promoting social inclusion in all dimensions of community life.

It is essential that the empowerment of local communities is not only seen as a short-term strategy, but as a long-term commitment. Relationships between businesses and local communities must be based on mutual trust and respect, and must be continually cultivated and strengthened. This means that companies must be willing to invest time, resources and effort in their relationships with local communities, and be patient in seeking results. True empowerment is not about quick fixes or immediate benefits, but rather about building a solid foundation for sustainable development that benefits everyone involved.

In short, empowering local communities is a key responsibility for companies that want to have a positive and sustainable impact. By creating employment opportunities, supporting education and entrepreneurship, protecting the environment, and promoting community engagement, businesses can contribute to the well-being and prosperity of the communities where they operate. This approach is not only beneficial for local communities, but also strengthens businesses, creating a more stable and favorable environment for their long-term success. In a world where connections between businesses and communities are increasingly important, community empowerment is not just a good practice, but a strategic necessity for any business that wants to thrive and leave a positive legacy.

Evelyn Wright

Ethics as a Pillar of Business Leadership

Ethics is one of the fundamental pillars of business leadership, and its importance cannot be underestimated. In a world where businesses have a significant influence on the economy, society and the environment, business leaders have a responsibility to act with integrity and do the right thing, even when no one is looking. Ethics in business is not only about complying with laws and regulations, but about adhering to moral principles and values that guide a company's decisions and actions. It is a commitment to honesty, transparency, respect and fairness, both within the company and in its relationship with the outside world.

An ethical business leader is noted for his or her ability to make decisions that are fair and equitable, not only for the company, but also for everyone who is affected by those decisions. This includes employees, customers, suppliers, the community and the environment. An ethical leader understands that business success cannot be achieved at the expense of others and that long-term prosperity is based on building relationships of trust and respect. Trust, once lost, is difficult to regain, and that is why acting ethically is crucial to maintaining the credibility and reputation of the company.

Ethics in business leadership begins with example. Leaders must be role models, demonstrating through their daily actions what it means to act with integrity. It is not enough to talk about the importance of ethics; Leaders must live those values in everything they do. This means making tough decisions when necessary, even if those decisions aren't the most popular or the most profitable in the short term. An ethical leader is willing to make sacrifices for the common good, knowing that, in the long term, this will benefit both the company and society.

One of the biggest challenges for business leaders is balancing business interests with ethical demands. In the business world, there is often constant pressure to maximize profits and minimize costs. However, a purely profit-oriented approach can lead to practices that are ethically questionable, such as labor exploitation, environmental damage or misleading advertising. An ethical leader recognizes these temptations and is committed to finding a balance between financial success and compliance with ethical principles. This may involve making decisions that seem less profitable in the short term, but in the long term preserve the integrity and sustainability of the company.

Ethics in leadership is also reflected in the way a company treats its employees. An ethical leader cares about the well-being of his team and ensures that all employees are treated with respect and dignity. This includes offering fair working conditions, adequate wages, and opportunities for professional development. It also means creating a work environment where diversity and inclusion are valued, and where all employees feel safe and supported. When employees feel like they are being treated fairly and respectfully, they are more likely to be engaged and motivated, which in turn benefits the company as a whole.

Transparency is another key aspect of ethics in business leadership. An ethical leader is open and honest in their communications, both inside and outside the company. Transparency builds trust and ensures that all stakeholders, from employees to shareholders to customers, have a clear understanding of the company's actions and decisions. Lack of transparency, on the other hand, can lead to distrust, confusion, and ultimately failure. In a world where information flows quickly and is easily accessible, transparency is not just a good practice, but a necessity to maintain a company's reputation and credibility.

Furthermore, ethics in business leadership extends to social and environmental responsibility. An ethical leader understands that the company does not operate in a vacuum and that it has a responsibility to contribute positively to society and to minimize its negative impact on the environment. This may include adopting sustainable practices, investing in local communities, and promoting equity and social justice. A leader who acts ethically in these areas not only improves the company's image, but also helps create a better world for future generations.

Accountability is another vital component of leadership ethics. An ethical leader is willing to accept responsibility for his or her decisions and actions, and does not seek to blame others when things go wrong. Accountability means being transparent about mistakes, learning from them, and taking steps to correct them. This attitude not only strengthens trust within the organization, but also shows employees and other stakeholders that the company is committed to continuous improvement and adherence to high ethical standards.

An ethical leader also understands the importance of fairness in business relationships. This means treating business partners, suppliers and customers fairly and equitably, and avoiding practices that may be perceived as exploitative or dishonest. Fairness is essential to building long-lasting and mutually beneficial business relationships. A leader who acts with fairness sets a tone of integrity that permeates the entire organization, fostering a culture of respect and responsibility.

Ethical decision making often requires a high degree of introspection and self-awareness. An ethical leader must be in tune with his or her own values and principles, and must be able to identify and resist pressures that could lead him to compromise those values. This can be particularly difficult in situations where personal or corporate interests appear to conflict with what is morally right. However, a truly ethical leader is willing to prioritize ethics over personal benefit or expediency, even when this means facing criticism or challenges.

Developing an ethical culture within the company is also the responsibility of leadership. Leaders must ensure that ethical values are a central part of the corporate culture, and this is achieved through constant communication, training, and the implementation of policies and procedures that reinforce those values. This also involves establishing and enforcing clear ethical standards, as well as creating an environment where employees feel comfortable reporting inappropriate conduct without fear of retaliation. A strong ethical culture not only protects the company from legal and reputational risks, but also fosters a more positive and productive work environment.

Ultimately, ethics as a pillar of business leadership is not just a matter of complying with external standards, but rather being in tune with an internal sense of what is right. Leaders who prioritize ethics not only lead their companies to financial success, they also contribute to a world where business can be a force for good. These leaders recognize that, at their core, companies are communities of people who depend on each other, and that the well-being of those people must be the primary objective of any business activity.

In conclusion, ethics is fundamental for business leadership, and its importance is reflected in all aspects of the management of a company. From decision making to creating a corporate culture, leaders who act with integrity and commitment to ethical principles not only build more successful companies, but also contribute to the well-being of society as a whole. As the world continues to change and challenges become more complex, the need for ethical leaders has never been more urgent. By focusing on ethics as an essential pillar of their leadership, entrepreneurs can ensure they are not only building a prosperous future for their companies, but also for the communities and planet we all share.

Evelyn Wright

Creating Shared Value

Creating shared value is a business philosophy that redefines the purpose of companies in society. Instead of focusing solely on maximizing profits for shareholders, this approach proposes that companies generate value for both society and themselves. The idea is simple but powerful: when a company addresses social and environmental issues as part of its business strategy, it not only benefits the community, but also drives its own success. This approach transforms the traditional perception of business by demonstrating that business interests and social well-being are not mutually exclusive, but are deeply intertwined.

The concept of shared value is based on the premise that business and society are interdependent. Companies need a prosperous society to have stable markets, trained employees and consumers with purchasing power. In the same way, society needs successful companies that generate employment, innovation and economic development. By aligning their business objectives with social needs, companies can unlock new growth opportunities, while contributing to solving problems such as poverty, unemployment, inequality and climate change. This approach not only creates a positive impact on society, but also strengthens the company's competitiveness and sustainability.

There are several ways companies can create shared value. One of them is through the reconception of products and markets. This involves developing products and services that not only meet consumer needs but also address social problems. For example, a food company may choose to produce healthier and more accessible foods, contributing to improved nutrition and public health. In this way, they not only capture a growing market, but also help solve a critical social problem. Likewise, companies can identify and serve segments of the population that have been underserved, creating products or services that meet their specific needs, while generating new sources of income.

Another way to create shared value is by redefining productivity in the value chain. This refers to improving the efficiency and effectiveness of business operations, while addressing social or environmental issues. For example, a company can reduce energy and water consumption in its production process, which not only decreases operating costs but also reduces environmental impact. Likewise, by improving the working conditions of its employees, a company can increase productivity, reduce employee turnover, and improve product quality. This approach not only improves the company's financial performance, but also creates a positive impact on the community and the environment.

Creating shared value can also be achieved by strengthening local communities. This involves collaborating with suppliers and local communities to improve their capacity and quality of life, which in turn strengthens the supply base and the stability of the company's operating environment. For example, a company that purchases raw materials from local producers can invest in training and technology to improve the productivity and quality of these producers' products. This not only ensures a stable and high-quality supply for the company, but also improves the income and well-being of local producers. This symbiotic relationship not only benefits the company, but also contributes to the economic and social development of the community.

The shared value approach should not be confused with traditional corporate social responsibility. While social responsibility often focuses on philanthropic or regulatory compliance activities, shared value is intrinsically tied to the company's business model. Rather than being a separate activity, shared value is integrated into the company's core strategy, seeking solutions that benefit both society and the company. It is a proactive approach that seeks business opportunities in solving social problems, rather than viewing these problems as external limitations or responsibilities.

A clear example of creating shared value is the company that invests in the training and education of its workforce. By offering continuous training programs, you not only improve the skills and competencies of your employees, increasing productivity and quality of work, but you also empower your employees, improving their employability and quality of life. In this way, the company benefits from a more trained and motivated workforce, while contributing to the professional and personal development of its employees, creating a positive impact on society in general.

Another example could be a company that invests in green technology to reduce its carbon footprint. By developing and using cleaner technologies, the company not only complies with environmental regulations and improves its reputation, but also reduces long-term operating costs and opens new market opportunities in environmentally conscious sectors. At the same time, it is contributing to the global fight against climate change, a problem that affects the entire society. This integration of business and social objectives is a perfect example of how shared value can be created effectively.

Creating shared value can also drive innovation within companies. In seeking solutions to social and environmental problems, companies are forced to think differently, question traditional methods and develop new ideas and approaches. This innovation not only solves social problems, but can also open new markets and improve the company's competitiveness. For example, a company that develops recyclable or biodegradable products is innovating not only in terms of sustainability, but also in creating new products that can appeal to environmentally conscious consumers.

Collaboration is another key aspect of shared value. No company can address all social and environmental problems alone. Therefore, collaboration with governments, non-governmental organizations, local communities and other businesses is essential to maximize impact. By working together, these parties can combine resources, knowledge and capabilities to develop more effective and sustainable solutions. For example, a company may partner with an NGO to implement an education program in a local community, where the company provides the financial and logistical resources, while the NGO offers its expertise in educational development. This collaboration not only creates value for the community, but also strengthens the company's relationship with the community and enhances its reputation.

The shared value approach also has the potential to transform entire industries. When multiple companies within a sector adopt the shared value approach, they can create systemic change that raises industry-wide standards. For example, if multiple companies within the food industry adopt sustainable agricultural practices, they not only improve the sustainability of their supply chains, but can also influence farmers, suppliers and competitors to adopt similar practices, creating a positive impact on the entire value chain. This collective shift not only benefits businesses, but also contributes to the long-term sustainability of the industry and the planet.

In short, creating shared value is a business approach that goes beyond traditional profits, aligning business interests with social and environmental needs. By developing products and services that address social problems, improving productivity in the value chain, strengthening local communities, driving innovation and collaborating with other stakeholders, companies can generate a positive impact on society, while strengthening their competitiveness and sustainability. This approach is not only beneficial for business and society, but also has the potential to transform entire industries and create a more just and sustainable world.

The Power of Collaboration

Collaboration is a powerful force that can transform companies, communities and entire societies. In the business world, working together toward a common goal can generate results that far exceed what a single entity could achieve alone. Collaboration is not simply about combining resources; It is about uniting minds, talents, ideas and efforts to create something greater and more meaningful. In an increasingly complex and globalized business environment, the ability to collaborate effectively has become an essential skill for long-term success.

The basis of effective collaboration is open and sincere communication. When people and organizations are willing to share information, ideas and resources, new opportunities for innovation and growth open up. Transparency in communication helps build trust, which is critical to any collaborative effort. Without trust, collaborations tend to fail because the parties involved become cautious and protective of their own interests. On the other hand, when trust is high, participants are more willing to take risks, share knowledge, and work together to overcome common challenges.

One of the greatest benefits of collaboration is the ability to leverage diversity of thought. When people from different backgrounds, experiences and skills come together, they bring unique perspectives that can lead to more creative and innovative solutions. In a collaborative team, ideas can be debated and refined, resulting in stronger decisions and more effective strategies. This diversity of thought is especially valuable in a business world where problems are increasingly complex and multifaceted. By joining forces, companies can address these challenges from multiple angles and find solutions that are more comprehensive and effective.

Collaboration also allows companies to share risks and resources. Instead of taking on the entire burden of a project or initiative, collaborating companies can spread the costs and risks among all parties involved. This not only reduces the financial and operational pressure on each individual company, but also increases the chances of success, as collaborations allow for the sharing of best practices, technologies and expertise. In a competitive environment, this ability to jointly share and leverage resources can make the difference between success and failure.

Another key aspect of collaboration is the creation of synergies. Synergies occur when collaboration produces a result that is greater than the sum of its parts. For example, two companies that come together to develop a new product may combine their individual strengths, such as the research and development expertise of one and the manufacturing capabilities of the other, to create a product that neither company could have developed independently. yes alone. This synergy not only speeds up the development process, but can also improve the quality of the final product and increase its success in the market.

Collaboration is not limited to relationships between companies. It can also occur within the same organization, between departments, teams and employees. In many companies, different departments often operate in silos, meaning they do not communicate or collaborate effectively with each other. This can lead to inefficiencies, duplication of effort, and missed opportunities. By fostering a culture of internal collaboration, companies can break down these silos and allow ideas, information, and resources to flow freely between all areas of the organization. This not only improves operational efficiency, but can also generate new opportunities for innovation and growth.

Furthermore, collaboration can extend beyond corporate boundaries and involve other stakeholders, such as governments, non-governmental organizations, local communities and consumers. In a world where social and environmental issues are increasingly pressing, collaboration between companies and other entities is essential to effectively address these challenges. For example, a company seeking to reduce its carbon footprint can collaborate with environmental organizations and local governments to develop sustainable solutions. This collaboration not only benefits the company, but also contributes to the well-being of society as a whole.

Collaboration also has the power to transform communities. When companies collaborate with local communities, they can help drive economic development, improve quality of life, and create opportunities for people. This may include initiatives such as job training programs, infrastructure projects, or community development efforts. By working closely with communities, companies not only create value for themselves, but also strengthen relationships with local residents and enhance their reputation as good corporate citizens.

However, for collaboration to be effective, it is crucial that all parties involved are aligned in their goals and expectations. This requires careful planning, clear communication, and a genuine commitment to mutual success. Successful collaborations don't happen by accident; They require a conscious effort to build and maintain strong relationships based on trust, respect and reciprocity. Companies must be willing to compromise, negotiate and find common ground where everyone can benefit.

A common challenge in collaborations is conflict management. When different parties work together, it is natural that disagreements and differences of opinion will arise. What is important is how these conflicts are handled. Successful collaborations are those in which conflicts are addressed constructively, with a focus on finding solutions that meet the needs of all parties. This requires effective communication skills, empathy, and the ability to see things from the perspective of others. When conflicts are managed well, they can strengthen collaboration by generating greater understanding and respect between the parties involved.

Collaboration also requires an open and flexible mindset. Companies and people involved in a collaboration must be willing to adapt to new ideas, methods and approaches. This may mean letting go of traditional ways of doing things and being open to experimenting and taking risks. Flexibility is especially important in an ever-changing business environment, where market conditions, technologies and consumer expectations can evolve rapidly. A successful collaboration is one that can adapt and evolve in response to these changes, taking advantage of the opportunities that arise in the process.

Finally, it is important to recognize and celebrate the achievements of collaboration. When a collaboration achieves its objectives, it is essential to recognize the effort and contribution of all parties involved. This not only strengthens the relationship and trust between collaborators, but also motivates everyone to continue working together on future projects. Celebrating success collaboratively also sends a positive message to the organization and society at large about the value and power of working together to achieve great things.

In short, the power of collaboration lies in its ability to unite people and organizations toward a common goal, leveraging diversity of thought, sharing risks and resources, and creating synergies that generate superior results. Collaboration can transform not only companies, but also communities and society at large. To be effective, collaboration requires open communication, trust, flexibility, and a genuine commitment to mutual success. In an increasingly interconnected and complex business world, collaboration is not just an option, but a necessity to achieve sustainable success and generate lasting positive impact.

Impact Measurement

Measuring the impact of a company's actions is essential to understand whether the decisions made are generating the desired results, both in business terms and in the social and environmental sphere. In a world where companies are increasingly committed to corporate social responsibility and sustainability, impact measurement has become an essential tool to evaluate progress, identify areas for improvement and demonstrate the value of responsible initiatives. Measuring impact is not just a matter of complying with regulations or satisfying stakeholders; It is a way to ensure that the company's actions are really making a difference.

Measuring impact begins with defining clear objectives. Without well-defined goals, it is impossible to know if the expected results are being achieved. These objectives must be specific, measurable, achievable, relevant and time-bound. For example, if a company decides to reduce its carbon footprint, it must establish a clear goal, such as reducing a certain percentage of emissions in a specific period. In this way, it can be evaluated if the implemented actions are leading towards the goal or if adjustments to the strategy are necessary.

Once the objectives have been defined, the next step is to identify key performance indicators, also known as KPIs. These indicators are the specific metrics that will be used to measure progress towards the objectives. KPIs must be relevant and directly linked to the established objectives. For example, if the goal is to improve employee health and well-being, a KPI could be a reduction in the number of sick days or an increase in participation in wellness programs. KPIs provide a quantitative way to assess impact, allowing the company to monitor and analyze results over time.

Data collection is an essential component of impact measurement. For measurement to be effective, data must be accurate, reliable, and collected regularly. This may involve implementing tracking and monitoring systems that capture relevant information in real time. For example, a company looking to reduce its energy consumption could install smart meters to track electricity usage in its facilities. The data collected can provide detailed insight into how initiatives are performing and where adjustments can be made to improve results.

Once data has been collected, it is important to analyze it systematically. Data analysis allows the company to identify trends, patterns and anomalies that can indicate whether actions are having the desired impact or if changes are required. This analysis may include comparing current results with established objectives, as well as with results from previous periods or with industry standards. Analysis can also help identify the underlying causes of problems and develop more effective solutions. For example, if a company finds that its waste reduction initiative is not achieving expected results, data analysis can reveal that certain processes or practices are not aligned with goals, which can guide the implementation of improvements.

Measuring impact is not just about numbers and statistics. It is also important to consider the qualitative impact of the company's actions. This may include the perception of employees, customers, communities, and other stakeholders about the company's initiatives. Surveys, interviews, and focus groups are useful tools for collecting this qualitative information. For example, a company implementing a volunteer program for its employees might conduct surveys to assess how employees perceive the value of the program and whether they feel they are making a difference in the community. This qualitative information provides a more complete view of impact and can complement quantitative data to provide a more holistic assessment.

Once the impact has been measured and analyzed, it is essential to communicate the results to all interested parties. Transparency in communication is key to maintaining the trust and commitment of employees, customers, investors and the community in general. Sustainability and corporate social responsibility reports are common tools for sharing this information. These reports should be clear, concise and accessible, presenting both successes and challenges honestly. Additionally, impact communication must be aligned with the company's strategy and values, demonstrating how actions are contributing to social and environmental well-being.

Measuring impact also gives companies the opportunity to continually learn and improve. By regularly reviewing results, companies can identify which initiatives are working well and which need to be adjusted. This constant feedback allows companies to be more agile and adapt quickly to changes in the environment or to the needs of interested parties. Additionally, measuring impact can inspire the company to set new, more ambitious goals as previous ones are achieved. This cycle of measurement, learning and continuous improvement is critical to sustainable growth and long-term success.

Measuring impact not only benefits the company, but also has a positive impact on society. When companies commit to measuring and improving their impact, they are contributing to a broader shift towards a more responsible and sustainable economy. This not only improves the company's reputation, but can also generate a multiplier effect, inspiring other companies to follow your example. Ultimately, impact measurement is a powerful tool for fostering a culture of responsibility and sustainability in the business world.

However, measuring impact is not without challenges. One of the main challenges is the complexity of measuring certain types of impact, especially those that are qualitative in nature or occur over the long term. For example, measuring the impact of a community empowerment initiative may be more difficult than measuring carbon emissions reduction. Additionally, some companies may face difficulties obtaining accurate and reliable data, especially in environments where data collection infrastructure is limited. Overcoming these challenges requires creativity, innovation and a genuine commitment to measuring impact.

Another challenge is ensuring that impact measurement is integrated and consistent across the organization. In many companies, responsibility for measuring impact may be dispersed across different departments or functions, which can lead to a lack of consistency and coordination. To overcome this, it is important that impact measurement is seen as a strategic priority at the corporate level, with a unified and coordinated approach. This may involve creating a dedicated team or allocating specific resources to ensure impact measurement is managed effectively.

In summary, impact measurement is an essential process to understand and improve the effect of a company's actions in the social, environmental and economic spheres. By setting clear objectives, identifying key performance indicators, collecting and analyzing data, and communicating results transparently, companies can ensure they are on the right path to making a positive impact. Although measuring impact can be challenging, it also offers an invaluable opportunity to learn, improve and contribute to the well-being of society. In a world where corporate responsibility and sustainability are increasingly important, measuring impact is not just an option, but a necessity for any company that aspires to be a force for positive change.

Preparing the New Generations of Entrepreneurs

Preparing new generations of entrepreneurs is a crucial task to ensure a future in which businesses not only prosper economically, but also contribute significantly to social and environmental well-being. Today, the business world is constantly changing, driven by technological advances, market transformations and greater awareness of the social and environmental impacts of business decisions. In this context, it is essential that future business leaders are equipped not only with technical skills and management knowledge, but also with a deep understanding of their responsibility towards society and the planet.

One of the first considerations when preparing new generations of entrepreneurs is education. Traditional business academic training has tended to focus on areas such as finance, marketing and operational management, which are undoubtedly important. However, in today's world, this knowledge alone is not enough. It is necessary to incorporate topics such as sustainability, business ethics, corporate social responsibility and change management into the study plans. These areas of knowledge help future entrepreneurs understand that the decisions they make in their businesses will have a much broader impact than simply the balance of profits and losses.

In addition to technical knowledge, it is essential to instill in new generations of entrepreneurs a mentality of purpose and values. Entrepreneurs of the future must be aware that business has a key role in building a more just and equitable society. This means acting with integrity, making ethical decisions, and considering the well-being of all stakeholders, not just shareholders. A company that operates with purpose has the potential to attract and retain talented employees, earn customer loyalty, and build strong relationships with the communities in which it operates.

Leadership is another essential aspect in the preparation of new generations of entrepreneurs. The business leaders of the future will need to be able to guide their teams in an environment of uncertainty and constant change. This requires developing skills such as resilience, empathy and the ability to inspire and motivate others. Leaders must be able to create a clear and compelling vision of the future, and communicate that vision in a way that inspires others to join them on their journey. They must also be able to make difficult decisions and take responsibility for their actions, always with a focus on the common good.

A key component in training entrepreneurs is the development of an innovative mindset. The ability to think creatively and look for new and disruptive solutions is essential in a world where industries are constantly evolving. Entrepreneurs must be willing to challenge the status quo, question traditional ways of doing business and explore new opportunities. Innovation is not just about creating new products or services; It also means finding more sustainable and effective ways of operating, reducing environmental impact and generating shared value for society.

Technology plays an increasingly important role in the business world, and new generations of entrepreneurs must be well versed in its use and potential. Digitalization, artificial intelligence, big data and other emerging technologies are transforming the way companies operate, interact with customers and make decisions. It is vital that future entrepreneurs not only understand how to use these technologies, but also how to ethically and responsibly integrate them into their businesses. This includes considering aspects such as privacy, equity in access to technology, and the social impact of technological decisions.

Another important aspect in preparing new generations of entrepreneurs is the understanding and management of diversity and inclusion. The business world is made up of people of different cultures, genders, ages and backgrounds, and taking advantage of this diversity is key to success. Entrepreneurs of the future must be able to create work environments where all voices are heard and valued, and where diversity is seen as a source of strength and creativity. Fostering an inclusive culture not only improves employee morale and productivity, but also allows companies to better connect with their customers and adapt to an increasingly diverse global market.

Globalization is another factor that new entrepreneurs must take into account. The business world is no longer limited by national borders; Companies operate in an interconnected global environment, where decisions made in one country can have repercussions in others. Future entrepreneurs must be prepared to operate in this global context, understanding the cultural, economic and regulatory differences that exist between different markets. Additionally, they must be aware of the social and environmental implications of their global operations, and be committed to creating value not only for their companies, but also for the communities in which they operate.

Corporate social responsibility (CSR) is a key area that must be integrated into the preparation of new entrepreneurs. Today, consumers and other stakeholders expect companies to not only focus on maximizing profits, but also contribute to the well-being of society. This includes practices such as fair trade, reducing our carbon footprint, philanthropy, and supporting local communities. Future entrepreneurs must understand that CSR is not just an additional component of their business strategy, but a fundamental aspect that can differentiate their company in a competitive market.

Business ethics is also a crucial component in training future business leaders. In an environment where business decisions can have a significant impact on society, it is essential that business owners act with integrity and transparency. This includes being honest with employees, customers and other stakeholders, as well as avoiding practices that may be harmful to society or the environment. Business ethics also involves being responsible in making decisions and being willing to be accountable for the company's actions.

Finally, the preparation of new generations of entrepreneurs must include the development of social and environmental awareness. Global challenges such as climate change, poverty, inequality and environmental degradation require companies to play an active role in finding solutions. The entrepreneurs of the future must be committed to creating business models that are sustainable and that contribute to the solution of these global problems. This may involve adopting more sustainable practices, innovating products and services that benefit the environment and society, and collaborating with other organizations and stakeholders to achieve positive impact.

In short, preparing new generations of entrepreneurs is not just a matter of imparting technical knowledge and management skills. It is a comprehensive process that requires instilling values, developing leadership skills, fostering innovation and creativity, and cultivating social and environmental awareness. Entrepreneurs of the future will need to be prepared to meet the challenges of an ever-changing world, and to do so in a way that not only generates economic benefits, but also contributes to the well-being of society and the planet. In doing so, they will be laying the foundation for a future where business is a powerful force for the common good, and where companies not only thrive, but also help build a more just, equitable and sustainable world.

Evelyn Wright

Towards a Regenerative Economy

The concept of a regenerative economy is gaining traction in the business and social world, and rightly so. At its core, it is about going beyond simply minimizing the damage that human activities cause to the planet and society. Rather than just reducing our negative impact, a regenerative economy seeks to create positive impact, restoring and improving the natural and social systems we depend on. This approach represents a radical change in the way we think about economic development and the role of business within it.

In a regenerative economy, the goal is not only to do less harm, but to regenerate natural resources and human communities that have been deteriorated by traditional economic activities. This means designing and operating businesses in ways that regenerate soil, restore biodiversity, revitalize communities and restore ecological balance. This approach recognizes that the planet's resources are not infinite and that if we continue to exploit them at the current rate, we will not only deplete those resources, but also cause irreversible damage to life-supporting systems.

To better understand this concept, it is useful to contrast it with the traditional linear economy approach, where resources are extracted, used to make products, and then disposed of. This "take, make, throw away" model has led to the overexploitation of natural resources and contributed to a global environmental crisis. In contrast, a regenerative economy takes a cyclical approach, inspired by natural processes, where waste is converted into resources and systems are continually regenerated. A clear example of this approach is regenerative agriculture, which seeks to restore soil health through practices such as crop rotation, the use of compost and the reduction of toxic chemicals, thus improving the soil's ability to sequester carbon and retain water.

The concept of regenerative economy also encompasses social and community dimensions. An economy that only cares about the environment, but ignores the needs and well-being of people, is not truly regenerative. In this sense, companies must strive to create jobs that are not only economically viable, but also meaningful and fair. This means paying decent wages, offering safe and respectful working conditions, and contributing to the development of local communities. In addition, companies must promote inclusion and equity, ensuring that the benefits of economic growth are distributed fairly among all people, regardless of their origin or social status.

A key element of the regenerative economy is innovation. To regenerate natural and social systems, we need to deeply rethink the way we do business. This means developing new technologies, products and business models that are not only sustainable, but also actively contribute to the regeneration of the environment. An example could be the manufacturing of products designed to last longer, be easily repaired or recycled at the end of their useful life, thus reducing the demand for natural resources and the generation of waste. Another example is the design of industrial processes that imitate natural cycles, where the byproducts of one activity become inputs for another, creating a closed and efficient system in the use of resources.

In addition to product and process innovation, the regenerative economy also requires a new way of thinking about value. In a linear economy, value is measured primarily in financial terms: how much money can be made from a transaction or investment. However, in a regenerative economy, value is also measured in terms of the environmental and social benefits generated. This means that companies must develop new metrics and tools to evaluate their performance, beyond the simple financial balance sheet. For example, they could measure the increase in biodiversity in the areas where they operate, the amount of carbon sequestered by their agricultural practices, or the improvement in the quality of life of local communities.

The transition to a regenerative economy is neither easy nor quick. It requires a profound change in the mindset of business leaders, governments and consumers. Entrepreneurs must be willing to question traditional business models and explore new ways of creating value. Governments must provide the appropriate regulatory framework and incentives to support this transition. And consumers must be aware of the consequences of their purchasing decisions and be willing to support companies that are committed to regeneration.

However, despite the challenges, the transition to a regenerative economy offers enormous opportunities. Companies that lead this change will not only contribute to the health of the planet and the well-being of people, but will also be better positioned to thrive in a world where natural resources are increasingly scarce and the pressure to act responsibly is high. ever increasing. Additionally, by creating value across multiple dimensions, these companies will be able to build stronger relationships with their customers, employees, and other stakeholders, giving them a competitive advantage in the long term.

A crucial aspect of the regenerative economy is collaboration. No company, government or organization can achieve regeneration alone. It is necessary for all actors to work together, sharing knowledge, resources and best practices. This may involve forming alliances between companies, collaborating with non-governmental organizations and actively participating in community initiatives. It can also mean creating support networks for small and medium-sized businesses, helping them adopt regenerative practices and access new markets. Collaboration is essential to scale regenerative solutions and to ensure that the benefits extend throughout society.

Education and awareness also play a fundamental role in the transition towards a regenerative economy. It is important that people understand the concepts and principles of regeneration, and feel empowered to act accordingly. This may include education in schools and universities, training in the workplace, and the dissemination of information through the media and social networks. By raising awareness of the regenerative economy, we can inspire more people to join this movement and contribute to positive change.

Finally, it is important to recognize that the regenerative economy is not a goal that can be achieved overnight. It is a continuous process of learning, adaptation and improvement. Companies and other organizations must be willing to experiment, make mistakes and learn from them. Regeneration is a journey, not a destination, and every step we take in the right direction brings us closer to a more sustainable and equitable future. This journey requires patience, perseverance and, above all, an unwavering commitment to the well-being of our planet and future generations.

In short, the regenerative economy is a bold and necessary vision for the future of business and society. By focusing on the regeneration of natural and social systems, rather than simply minimizing damage, this approach offers a new way of understanding and practicing economic development. Although the transition to a regenerative economy presents challenges, it also offers enormous opportunities for companies willing to lead the change. Through innovation, collaboration, and a focus on long-term value, we can build a future where business thrives in ways that benefit every living thing on our planet.